30 M...
... To Solve That Problem

Michael Stevens

**KOGAN
PAGE**

YOURS TO HAVE AND TO HOLD

BUT NOT TO COPY

First published in the UK by Kogan Page, 1998

Kogan Page Limited
120 Pentonville Road
London N1 9JN

British Library Cataloguing in Publication Data
A CIP record for this book is available from the British Library.

ISBN 0 7494 2781 7

Typeset by The Florence Group, Stoodleigh, Devon

Printed and bound in Great Britain by Clays Ltd, St Ives plc

CONTENTS

The 30 Minutes Series

The *Kogan Page 30 Minutes Series* has been devised to give your confidence a boost when faced with tackling a new skill or challenge for the first time.

So the next time you're thrown in at the deep end and want to bring your skills up to scratch or pep up your career prospects, turn to the *30 Minutes Series* for help!

Titles available are:

30 Minutes Before Your Job Interview

30 Minutes Before a Meeting

30 Minutes Before a Presentation

30 Minutes to Boost Your Communication Skills

30 Minutes to Brainstorm Great Ideas

30 Minutes to Deal with Difficult People

30 Minutes to Succeed in Business Writing

30 Minutes to Master the Internet

30 Minutes to Make the Right Decision

30 Minutes to Make the Right Impression

30 Minutes to Plan a Project

30 Minutes to Prepare a Job Application

30 Minutes to Write a Business Plan

30 Minutes to Write a Marketing Plan

30 Minutes to Write a Report

30 Minutes to Write Sales Letters

Available from all good booksellers.
For further information on the series, please contact:

Kogan Page, 120 Pentonville Road, London N1 9JN
Tel: 0171 278 0433 Fax: 0171 837 6348

INTRODUCTION

Problem solving is a common everyday activity: getting the car going when it won't start; finding out what led to a customer complaint; choosing the best PC and software for use at home; completing a difficult task to a short dead-line; even getting the job you want.

Problem solving means finding the best way to get successfully from A to B. It is not a mystical process that requires special skills. It is an everyday activity carried out by everyone, often without thinking.

Every day we come across situations where it is difficult to achieve what we want, or where we are uncertain what to do. We may have many options but not know which one to choose. We may know some of the answers, or none of them. Problem solving helps us deal with the situation, by bridging the gap between how things are and how we would like them to be.

We use problem solving to put things right when they go wrong. We also use it to help us improve the way we do things, and to achieve things we, and sometimes others, have never done before. It helps us to exploit opportunities.

In competitive situations we should always be trying to make improvements. Innovation through problem solving helps people and businesses find more efficient ways to operate and adapt to rapid change. Good problem solvers adapt more quickly to change. They can make better use of their knowledge and skills and generally achieve more.

Problem solving is a skill that develops naturally as we grow up and learn. We do not often see how it is working, but it is there in the background helping us deal from day to day with life's problems, both at work and in our personal life.

If you understand how your mind is working when you solve problems, you will be able to improve the way you do it. This book will help you to do that. It provides practical advice on how to:

- recognize and overcome some common hindrances to problem solving;
- use specific techniques to help with different types of problem;
- generate a wider range of possible solutions;
- evaluate different solutions to identify the best solution;
- ensure that solutions are implemented properly.

Some problems can be resolved with relative ease, while others present a greater challenge, which may require prolonged effort and concentration. Whatever the circumstances, becoming a better problem solver is rewarding in many ways. Good problem solvers are able to:

- foresee certain problems and take preventive action;
- resolve problems more quickly and with less effort;
- reduce stress;

- improve their work performance and working relation-ships;
- create and exploit opportunities;
- solve more demanding problems;
- exert greater control over key aspects of their lives;
- gain greater personal satisfaction.

Make better use of your natural problem-solving abilities by spending 30 minutes reading this book. Whatever your longer-term personal and professional goals, a growing sense of personal effectiveness will ensure that you gain quick payback from the effort.

1

SEEING PROBLEMS CLEARLY

To solve problems effectively, and put your skills to best use, you first need to be aware of a problem when it exists, and to see it as it really is.

Not all problems are obvious even when they affect us. We may be unaware of a disagreement between two colleagues at work, for example, but it can still affect our work as part of the team. Also, not all problems are what they seem. The brain is excellent at filtering out information that is not essential. We respond automatically to many situations, relying on just a small sample of information. For example, if we receive a document of four pages numbered one, two, four and five, we might assume that page three is missing. On looking more closely, we might find that the pages were in fact numbered incorrectly, and that they are all there.

To help you solve problems you need:

- methods to help you recognize problems; and

- ways to make sure you have all the information about a problem.

Recognizing problems

There are two main types of problem. *Maintenance* problems are those where the current situation is not what it should be. It can be the result of something failing to happen as it should (the car doesn't start), or something happening that should not (a wheel falls off).

The second type are *achievement* problems, where the current situation could be better, but there are reasons why it is not. Achievement problems can be divided into three groups:

- where a goal or objective has not been achieved; for example, failing to complete a task on time;

- where the objective could be exceeded; for example, completing eight calls in an hour instead of the required five;

- where an opportunity exists; for example, finding a new way of doing something that cuts the time required in half.

It is important to make the distinction between the two types of problem. It shows that problem solving is not only about putting things right when they go wrong. It can also help us to set targets or goals, in order to improve our performance and exploit opportunities.

Problems are not always obvious or tangible. Sometimes they have little immediate impact. What we think is a problem may turn out not to be a problem at all. Some problems change over time, becoming more or less important, or even disappearing altogether. Others arise suddenly, without warning, and are obvious by their effects.

The following situation highlights how some problems develop. A company has a very busy department engaged in processing orders, mostly from other small companies. When the company wins two big orders, the staff cannot cope; the manager decides to hire more staff, but that takes time. The processing of some orders is therefore delayed. The department's objective is to process orders as they arrive. Normally, there are enough staff and hours in the day to do this sufficiently quickly. When the two new orders dramatically increase the workload, the objective or target has become much bigger. An obstacle has arisen that prevents the department achieving its objective.

A problem arises when an obstacle prevents the achievement of an objective. Obstacles and objectives can increase or decrease in size. These changes can determine how, and even if, a problem is tackled. If objectives or targets are monitored for change, and potential obstacles identified, action can often be taken, either to prevent a problem occurring, or at least to make sure that everyone is prepared to tackle the problem as soon as it arises.

Identifying the areas in which problems might occur, and establishing methods of detecting them, helps you to recognize problems efficiently. Having your car serviced regularly, for example, should give you advance warning to replace worn components. At work, performance monitoring detects shortfalls in the achievement of targets and standards. Observing and listening to others helps to detect changes that may reflect an underlying problem.

A systematic approach also helps you to recognize opportunities for improvement. Ask yourself if you could exceed the targets or standards set for you, and whether there are new goals you could set yourself.

Remember, it is important not to jump to conclusions about apparent problems and their possible causes. Situations can be deceptive.

Seeing problems as they really are

Many hidden factors may affect our problem solving, some exist in our psychological make-up (personal factors), and some in our surroundings (outside factors). It is mostly these factors, rather than our ability, that stop us being better problem solvers.

Personal factors

We do not usually think about how we solve problems, because it comes naturally, and few people receive specialist training in problem solving. These two factors are a disadvantage when it comes to solving more difficult problems. When you understand the skills involved, which are outlined in this book, you will be able to use them more effectively.

As we grow up we learn ways of thinking that may distort our view of problems. Because the brain relies only on partial information to recognize common situations, we tend to see what we *expect* to see. We jump to conclusions, based on the obvious signs, and look no further.

Another consequence of relying on partial information is that sometimes we may not recognize that a problem exists. The fact that an account tallies, for example, does not necessarily rule out fraud. Opportunities can also be missed when we do not see the full picture.

Here are some tips to help you avoid these difficulties:

- establish procedures that will alert you to problems and opportunities;
- do not rely on single or obvious measures to classify a problem;
- question whether you have all the facts or whether you are making assumptions;
- know clearly what you want to achieve, so that you can recognize opportunities when they arise.

When solving problems, we manipulate ideas in our head as well as perhaps talking to others about them, putting ideas on paper and acting. We use a range of 'languages' for these activities, mostly words and symbols. Mathematical and chemical equations are examples of specialist languages that may help to manipulate ideas and explain and solve problems.

Not all problems are best tackled using words. Explaining how to get by car from A to B, for example, is often much easier if we draw the route or point it out on a map.

Just as you may be unable to understand someone who does not speak your language, you might encounter difficulties if you cannot use the language best suited to a particular problem. Even if we understand the language, we may not use it. Because we express ourselves so much in words, we tend to use them automatically to describe and solve problems, even when there is an easier way.

To avoid these difficulties, you might try the following:

- think about which language is most likely to help you with a particular problem;
- get help if you need to use a particular language and have difficulty with it;
- try using different languages; for example, visuals instead of words, or charts instead of rows of numbers.

Emotion exerts a powerful influence over thoughts and actions. The brain uses emotions to encourage behaviour that is 'good' for us, physically and mentally. This gives rise to emotional 'needs', such as the desire for achievement, order and self-esteem. If these needs conflict with our situation, we may find it difficult to act in an appropriate way. All this happens unconsciously and can hinder problem solving.

Fear of looking foolish in front of others is common. It makes us stick with things we know. Many people fear taking risks, when the outcome is uncertain or could be unpleasant. As a result, we tend to set objectives within easy reach and accept solutions we know will be successful. Exploring unusual ideas and suggesting risky solutions is an important step towards finding the best solution.

Avoiding anxiety is another common hindrance. In order to avoid becoming anxious we may avoid taking risks, be indecisive in ambiguous situations, and avoid challenging the status quo. All these factors can have a negative effect on problem solving.

Wanting to bring order to a situation or to gain recognition through success can make us impatient to solve a problem. Impatience can lead us to grab the first workable solution and automatically reject unusual ideas.

Emotion is deep-seated. It is not easy to change but it will help you with problem solving if you can try the following:

- question existing ideas and methods;

- accept that, if you are looking for new and better ways of doing things, some mistakes are almost inevitable;

- try to develop unusual ideas to a practical level before showing them to anyone;

13

- follow a methodical approach to curb impatience;
- tackle big problems in small manageable steps.

Outside factors

Our surroundings can affect the way we feel, think and work. The type of situation we favour for problem solving varies, depending on what puts us in the right frame of mind. Some people thrive in a bustling atmosphere, while others prefer quieter surroundings. Quiet may be more conducive to logical analytical thinking, whereas lively surroundings might help us get into a more relaxed, free-thinking frame of mind. We learn from experience what conditions suit us best for different types of mental task.

Outside stimuli – noise, heat, cold, light – affect our level of mental alertness. Up to a point, this helps us concentrate. After that, our thinking can become fuzzy. Emotions such as frustration and anger also affect us. There are no hard and fast rules. You know best what makes you alert and what puts you in a more relaxed and free-thinking frame of mind.

At work, several factors may affect our problem solving. We follow a set of guidelines – formal and informal rules. We work with other people, each with their own way of doing things. We have targets to achieve and standards to maintain. Being told to do things in a certain way makes it difficult to find better ways of working.

Some companies use suggestion schemes because they know staff are a good source of money-saving and money-making ideas. Good managers are always open to new ideas. They encourage people to develop their ideas into practical solutions, offering constructive criticism when it is needed. They reward people for good ideas, with praise and recognition, and sometimes with bonuses for working more efficiently.

There is not much you can do to change your work environment, but you can try the following in order to avoid some of its negative effects:

- do not assume that things have to be done in a certain way just because that is how they have always been done;

- make it your business to find out if the company has a suggestion scheme;

- if people always criticize new ideas, work out the benefits and a practical plan to implement your solution before you suggest it;

- just because other people do not seem to be interested in finding better ways of working, do not assume that there are no opportunities to do so;

- if your work is not challenging enough, set yourself personal targets that stretch you.

Think about your reactions and thought processes when you tackle problems, and about how outside factors influence you, and use the techniques suggested to overcome negative effects.

2

DEFINING PROBLEMS

Before you attempt to solve a problem, you need to know what is causing it, or what it is you want to achieve.

The first sign that a problem exists is often a hazy notion that things are not as they should be, or that they could be better. To deal with the situation effectively you need to describe or define it as something upon which you can act. Problem definitions vary in complexity but they point you in the right direction for further work on the problem. This is an important step, and if you spend time doing it properly you will find your problem solving much easier later.

To define a problem, you need information. The knowledge that there is a problem is part of this information. Perhaps you have noticed that when you drag your PC mouse, the cursor jumps instead of moving smoothly. This suggests what type of further information you need, and gives you an idea of where to look for it. You may need to redefine a problem, perhaps several times, as you under-stand more about the situation. You might explore the possibility of dirt clogging the mouse. If that turns out to be wrong, you might go on to look for a loose connection.

Maintenance and achievement problems are usually defined in different ways, so you need first to decide which type of problem you have. Remember, maintenance prob-lems are the result of something failing to happen as it should, or of something happening that should not. In achievement problems, the current situation could be better, but there are reasons why it is not.

Maintenance problems

In maintenance problems, the emphasis is on identifying and specifying possible causes. In a maintenance problem there is deviation from the norm. You start to define the problem by identifying and recording all the deviations. From these, you can begin to identify possible causes.

One technique used to define a maintenance problem helps you systematically analyse and define all the circum-stances surrounding it. It consists of answering a series of questions such as:

- What is the problem? What isn't the problem?
- Where is the problem? Where isn't the problem?
- What is distinctive about it?
- Who/what does the problem involve? Who/what doesn't it involve?
- When did/does the problem occur? When didn't/doesn't it occur?
- What is the same/different when the problem occurs?
- Is the problem getting bigger/smaller?

Questions can be adapted so that all known facts about the problem are identified. Once the situation has been fully documented, possible causes may be apparent. These are tested against the known facts and the actual cause is the one that would lead to precisely the effects seen. This is very much like the logical deductions you make automatically when you think about why something has happened. Often, you have to hypothesize other possible causes; you can use idea-generation techniques (see Chapter 4) for this.

Once the actual cause of a maintenance problem is identified, the action required may be obvious and straightforward. A faulty PC mouse can be replaced, for example.

Achievement problems

Achievement problems are defined in terms of objectives (what you want to achieve), and the obstacles standing in your way. The definition needs to be precise, to give clear direction to your search for solutions, and, at the same time, identify all possible goals that would contribute to your overall objective. For example, achieving many separate goals may improve your chances of promotion.

Achievement problems often do not have a single 'correct' definition, so they are best defined in two stages – first, exploring all the possible goals and then defining precisely which ones you want to achieve. Then the obstacles to achieving these goals are specified.

'How to . . . ?' statements are useful for thinking of alternative goals and routes to a solution. 'How to increase my chances of promotion?', for example, could be re-stated as 'How to make me more valuable to my employer?' or 'How to become more efficient?' or 'How to improve my skills?' or 'How to find a job where my skills are more useful?'.

There is also usually more than one way of looking at a problem. What appears to be a single problem may in fact be a collection of related problems. You can use some of the techniques described in Chapter 4 to create alternative 'How to . . . ?' statements and goals.

The more precise your definition, the better your chances of finding an effective solution. 'How to improve my job prospects?' does not tell you where to look for solutions. If you define it in terms of specific goals, such as 'How, within three months, to extend my school Spanish vocabulary to include business terminology?', your problem solving will be more efficient. This statement defines your situation now, your goal and the gap you need to bridge.

The same is true of statements about obstacles. The more clearly you can define them, the easier it is to deal with them. Ask yourself questions such as:

- What is the obstacle?

- How did/does it arise?

- What are its dimensions?

- What are its effects?

- Is it growing or diminishing?

Obstacles to improving your Spanish vocabulary could include lack of incentive, lack of time, no knowledge of suitable courses, lack of practice, and the number of business terms you need to learn.

To write a detailed problem definition, first select the 'How to . . . ?' statements that most accurately represent the problem. Then, for each one, write down the characteristics of the current situation and the desired situation. Whenever possible, state these in measurable terms, so that you know what will constitute a successful solution, when it should be achieved, and how you will measure your success. Next, add details of any obstacles and how they prevent you reaching your objective. This forms the basis for your search for solutions. Try it out using an example such as 'How to make better use of my time so that I have six hours a week to . . . ?'.

Sometimes, your actions in solving a problem will affect other people. If you are going to spend six hours a week learning a new skill, will it mean spending less time with friends and family? Depending on the situation, you can either modify your objectives, or set secondary objectives in order to accommodate the needs of others. Maybe you could get your friends to go on a course with you, so that you can offer each other support.

You can use the following checklist to review how thoroughly you have defined a problem.

- Can this objective be divided into several sub-goals?
- Is this objective the ultimate goal in solving the problem?
- Are there other related objectives?
- Can this obstacle be sub-divided?
- Are there other related obstacles?
- Does this obstacle prevent me reaching other objectives?
- Does this definition take account of the needs of others who are involved or affected?

You can use the techniques for defining achievement problems to help define maintenance problems once you know their cause. Sometimes, the process of defining a problem reveals that it does not require action, perhaps because it will disappear and not recur, or because the actual loss or potential gain is insignificant.

Is action necessary?

The effects of some problems are not significant enough to warrant time and effort in solving them. Even when they are, because many objectives and obstacles go through phases of growing and shrinking, tackling a problem immediately may not be the best course of action. You have four main options when you encounter a problem:

- do nothing; for example, when the problem is likely to solve itself, when its effects are insignificant, or when the cost of solving it is greater than the potential gains;

- monitor the situation; for example, when it is not urgent, when the problem is diminishing, when you are unsure of the cause, when you need time to plan what to do, or when the obstacle is getting smaller;

- deal with the effects; for example, when the cause will subside, when the cost of removing the cause is too great, or when an obstacle is too immovable;

- try to solve it immediately; for example, when the problem is growing, when it is having serious effects, when the obstacle is getting larger, or when there is an imminent deadline.

Common sense will usually tell you whether you need to act or not. If you do decide to act, the search for solutions involves finding ways to close the gap between your current situation and one in which you will have achieved your objective. First, though, you need to fully understand the problem.

3

UNDERSTANDING
A PROBLEM

Some problems require no further analysis once you have defined them. The definition of a maintenance problem, for example, might confirm that the hard disk drive in your PC has failed. Replacing it, and the data on it, solves the problem. More complex problems, such as the PC crashing on a regular basis, require further analysis to help identify how to bridge the gap between the current and the desired situations. Achievement problems generally require most work at this stage.

Before starting detailed work on a problem, decide if you should involve others. This may mean people who are part of the problem or affected by it, with experience or knowledge of this type of problem, or people with the resources needed to solve it. The list of questions on pages 36–7 will help you decide.

Explore and analyse the problem

Thorough information forms the basis for developing effective solutions. You must distinguish between facts, ideas, needs and opinions, although all may be important.

Analysing maintenance problems can result in a vast amount of information; this can be used to eliminate causes that do not fit the facts. As causes are eliminated you may need to gather more information about the remaining possibilities. Through a cyclical process of investigation and elimination you eventually identify the actual cause.

The definition of achievement problems gives clues about what is relevant – the current and desired situations and obstacles – and where such information might be found. The following questions can be useful:

- What specific information is required; for example, dates, times, amounts, names, actions?

- Why is this information required – to eliminate possibilities, confirm hunches, identify resources for solving the problem?

- What are the sources of this information?

- What form will it take; for example, numerical, statistical, verbal, physical evidence?

- How accurate or reliable are the sources?

- Where can this information be obtained?

Try to gather and record information systematically. If necessary, verify the original source and how and when it was gathered. Remember that numerical and statistical data can be manipulated.

You can use the methods for representing problems described below, and the idea-generation techniques in Chapter 4, to help identify relevant information.

Representing a problem

Models

A crucial aspect of problem solving, especially with complex problems, is how you organize and represent information. Two very common difficulties are not seeing all the relationships between different parts of a problem and not seeing beyond the most obvious solution. It helps to have a tangible representation of the problem – a model – to give structure to the information. Models help to do the following:

- reveal relationships between different parts of a problem;

- highlight gaps in your information and understanding;

- stimulate your search for solutions;

- communicate the problem to other people;

- predict the likely consequences of actions you think might solve the problem.

There are many different types of model, composed variously of words, graphics, mathematical formulae, and symbols, as well as physical models.

Various standard models are used to represent problems which have common elements linked by the same relationships. These can be applied to any problem that fits the model. The common elements in communication are the originator, the sender, the message, the medium and the receiver. Effective communication relies on an efficient flow of information from one end to the other. This model can be used to analyse communication in a particular situation and identify exactly what is happening at each stage. Some other types of model are described below.

Word descriptions

Words are the simplest and one of the most popular and flexible ways of representing a problem, either alone, or in combination with pictorial or graphical elements. The easiest way to create a word model is to list the main features of a problem and update the list as other ideas spring to mind. Word models can be manipulated, by putting words in sequence or classifying them into groups, in order to highlight relationships and differences in the information.

Giving structure to information in word models can be difficult, so it is a good idea to use word models in combination with other types of model.

Drawings and diagrams

Drawing is an ideal way of beginning to create some kind of structure with your ideas. Lines and shapes can represent relationships and give concrete form to a problem. Drawings can suggest new relationships, new ways of structuring a problem and new routes to a solution.

A 'mind map' is a method of recording ideas that stimulates creative thinking. Start by writing down the main idea or concept, and then add ideas as they spring to mind, represented as branches off this central point. Label each branch so it can trigger recall of associated ideas, and keep adding branches until you have exhausted all your ideas.

Branches are not limited to straight lines. A wavy line might represent fluctuation, for example, and an expanding spiral something escalating out of control. Do not impose structure consciously; relationships will emerge through the association of ideas.

Chain diagrams, such as flowcharts, are created in a more logical way and show in sequence how the main elements of a problem are related. You could show the stages in the manufacture of a product, for example, with the materials, labour and time input at each stage.

You can show alternative choices and the influence of chance events to create a tree diagram. When numbers are added to show the value of choices and the probability of chance events, a decision tree is created, which you can use to evaluate alternative courses of action.

A fault-tree diagram is another variation, which helps to identify the causes of a problem. You start with the problem (for example, figures do not tally), which branches into possible primary causes (error in calculation, data incorrect); these are further sub-divided according to their possible causes (faulty calculator, carelessness, error in transcription, error in collection).

Force field diagrams are an analytical tool for graphically representing the equilibrium between opposing forces and suggesting ways of influencing them. Applied to a problem, a line down the centre of a page represents the problem situation – the current equilibrium. On one side are the forces or actions that would push equilibrium in the direction required to achieve your objective. On the other are the opposing or restraining forces that act against the desired change – obstacles that must be weakened, removed or overcome to solve the problem.

Force field analysis can be divided into simple stages:

1. Describe the current situation.
2. Describe the objective or desired outcome.
3. Describe the least desired outcome (a worsening of the problem).
4. Draw the basic diagram.
5. Identify the driving forces (those acting to push equilibrium towards the objective).

6. Identify the opposing or restraining forces.

7. Add these to the diagram.

8. Identify neutral forces; these are not active now but could become driving or opposing forces when action is taken, or when the equilibrium is disturbed.

9. Describe individual forces in detail and rate their relative importance or strength.

10. Rate the ease of changing each force.

11. Select the forces to be changed.

12. Look for ways of influencing these forces as required.

This technique is useful particularly where human factors are important, such as in behavioural problems and changes in working practices or systems.

Mathematical models

Problems involving quantitative information need to be represented in number terms, even if only to record the data. Mathematical models can represent relationships between elements of a problem and provide a means of manipulating them: for example, $A + B = C$. Constructing simple mathematical models is relatively easy, and some highly complex models are available on PCs to non-mathematicians. These can help to solve a wide range of problems by analysing a situation and forecasting how various actions, changes or forces will affect it. One example is financial modelling with a spreadsheet package.

Using an appropriate method to represent a problem will often suggest some ideas for a solution. Other techniques for generating ideas are described in Chapter 4.

What is an effective solution?

Before developing solutions, you need to know what will constitute an effective solution. Sometimes there will be both 'acceptable' and 'ideal' outcomes and you can define both. Make a detailed list of what you want to achieve and what factors must be taken into account in the solution. Begin by asking yourself the following questions:

- What benefits am I seeking?

- What obstacles/causes do I have to deal with?

- What are the constraints on the situation (time, space, people, materials)?

- What will be acceptable to others affected by the problem/solution? To others who have to agree to the solution? To others who will provide the necessary resources? To others who have to implement the solution?

- What are the risk factors and what level of risk is acceptable?

Some of these questions can only be answered fully after you have devised possible solutions. These 'criteria of effectiveness' give direction to your search for solutions, and will help you later to compare the relative effectiveness of different solutions (*see* Chapter 6). The criteria are not set in stone, however, because you may find a solution that warrants changing the constraints. Spending 20 per cent more time on something to gain a 50 per cent better outcome, for example, would be a worthwhile trade-off.

4

DEVISING SOLUTIONS

Devising solutions can be exciting. Achievement problems, in particular, give you the opportunity to use your imagination and explore seemingly outlandish ideas to form the basis of a practical solution.

At this stage, you are looking for a course of action that leads as near as possible to the ideal solution. The direct route, however, is not always the easiest. Just as when you have something on the tip of your tongue, and the harder you try to remember it, the more remote it seems, concentrating on the outcome you want can make it harder to come up with the solution to a problem.

Creating ideas

Your best approach is to create as many ideas as possible related to achieving your objective, and then to test them to see if they give the results you want. This way, you are not limiting yourself to commonplace solutions that could be bettered.

Analysing the problem should have provided you with a large amount of information and possible ideas with which to work. Continually questioning your view of the situation as you search for solutions will inspire you to explore all the possibilities. For example, you might ask yourself some of the following questions:

- Do I really need to achieve this objective?
- Could I substitute a different objective?
- Could I achieve this objective in a different way?
- Would there be any advantage in delaying trying to achieve this objective?
- Is this really an obstacle?
- Can I side-step this obstacle?
- Can I use this obstacle to my advantage?

As you construct different plans of action, you can use an appropriate model to represent how each action con- tributes to achieving your overall objective. Models also help you predict the effects of various actions and to see how they interact. It is important that the actions form a coherent strategy for tackling the problem. When several actions have to run consecutively, for example, you need to ensure that together they will meet any time constraints, and that there are no conflicting demands on resources.

Each action you propose will be intended to achieve a particular effect, but it can also have side-effects that may be desirable or undesirable. Try to build into your solutions ways to minimize undesirable side-effects and to enhance desirable ones. Introducing new technology to improve effi- ciency, for example, may necessitate training. In turn, this could be an opportunity to reorganize associated out-dated processes and procedures.

Identify all the factors that could influence the effectiveness of your solution by asking yourself these questions:

- What could go wrong?
- Are there related factors over which I have no control?
- Could this objective change?
- Could this obstacle become more obstinate?
- Could relevant new obstacles arise?
- Might this action create new opportunities that I could exploit at the same time?

There are basically five sources of ideas for solving a problem, and you should use as many of the following as possible:

- past experience of similar situations;
- logical deduction from the facts;
- other people;
- published sources;
- creative idea-generation techniques.

It can be difficult to see beyond the obvious, especially when you are under pressure. You can use various techniques to give you a fresh perspective on a situation and to generate ideas for solutions. These techniques work by helping you combine information or ideas in ways you might not otherwise consider. The result is a large number of ideas, some of which may be useful as the basis for solving a problem.

An important rule in using many of these techniques is not to evaluate ideas. That comes later. Judging whether ideas may be useful hinders the process of combining information in unusual and potentially useful ways. The rule is to think in a 'playful' way and deliberately suspend judgement.

Techniques for fluency and flexibility

The more ideas you can produce, the more fluent your thinking. The more wide-ranging your ideas, the more flexible your thinking. Fluency and flexibility are important in problem solving, and the following techniques help to improve both when you are thinking about a problem.

Free association

With this technique, you allow your mind to wander without deliberate direction. You name the first thought that comes to mind in response to a word, symbol, idea or picture associated with the problem, then use that thought as a trigger, quickly repeating the process over and over to produce a stream of associations. It is important to avoid justifying the connection between successive ideas. Free association delves deep into the memory, helping to uncover remote relationships between ideas. The ideas need to be recorded either on paper or on audio tape.

Discussion

A simple way of getting additional ideas on a problem is to discuss it with other people. They will often have a different perspective on the problem and its implications, and different values and ideals. Even if they cannot contribute significant ideas directly, what they say may trigger new lines of thought for you.

Daydreaming

Daydreaming is often frowned upon and discouraged as a serious thinking skill. It is considered fanciful, indulgent and unproductive. In fact, it can be very useful. As the name implies, it allows you time out for playful, uninhibited thinking. It is private, so your ideas can be as outlandish as you like. There is no risk, because it involves only thought, and not action. It can involve feelings and emotions, which add a valuable dimension to your thinking. Ideas can be manipulated quickly and potential obstacles foreseen. Rewards can be envisaged and this can act as a motivator. It helps to develop plans that prepare you to look out for information and opportunities to help you achieve your objectives.

Productive daydreaming has to be directed towards a particular goal; it is often called 'wishful thinking'. You can use it to help you build plans for achieving your goals.

Visualizing

Thinking about a problem in visual terms can be useful in solving many types of problem. If you had to calculate the amount of carpet required to cover a spiral staircase, for example, you would probably automatically picture the staircase in your mind. From there, you would start to devise ways to make the calculation, based on the shape of the steps. The choice may not always be so obvious, but visualizing is a powerful and flexible way of thinking about problems, and the skill can be developed with practice.

Take a break

When you are stuck with a problem after working on it for some time, it is often productive to take a break. You can reach a stage where your thinking becomes fixed on certain ideas, and you cannot 'see the wood for the trees'. When time allows, putting a problem aside for a while can give you a new perspective.

Bug lists and wish lists

These are simply lists of things that cause you irritation or dissatisfaction (bug lists), and things you would like to change or achieve (wish lists). They are a useful and fun way to search for opportunities to improve your performance at work, aim for promotion and increase your satisfaction with life.

Combination techniques

Various techniques require you to combine unrelated objects or ideas, to see if there is a new, practical outcome. This kind of activity has led to the production of a number of commercial items, such as the multi-purpose workbench and the Swiss Army knife.

One combination technique is attribute listing, which is used to identify ways to improve something. It consists of three stages:

1. describe the physical attributes or characteristics of each component of the item or system;

2. describe the functions of each component;

3. examine each component in turn, to see if changing its attributes would bring about an improvement in its function.

One example is a screwdriver. The simple original version has been improved by the addition of numerous variations, including a filament for current detection, multiple screw-in shafts, magnetic blades and ratchet mechanisms.

Attribute listing can also be used to search for alternative areas in which a product or service could be used, by looking for applications for individual attributes. The attributes of optical fibres, for instance, have made them useful in fields as diverse as telecommunications, medicine and exhibition lighting.

Morphological analysis is a similar technique. A simple method of carrying out such analysis is to do the following:

1. list the parameters of the situation;
2. sub-divide each into its smallest parts;
3. represent these parts in a matrix;
4. examine all possible combinations of these parts.

A simple way to represent each component is to draw a three-dimensional cube and divide it into many smaller cubes. Along the edges of the cube, write one component in each square. Each small cube can represent a combination of six different components. Try it using the following simple example (or your own). List the various options for motivating people at work. Along one side, list the different behaviours that can be rewarded, one per square. Then list how they can be rewarded and then how often they can be rewarded. You will see how the forced combination suggests ideas you may not otherwise have imagined.

The best idea-generation technique to use is often determined by the type of problem and what you are trying to achieve. In situations where you have a choice, practice will tell you which techniques will work best for you. With practice, these techniques will become less mechanical and time-consuming.

5

WORKING TOGETHER

A lot of problem solving takes place in group settings. Meetings and informal discussions are used to air ideas and points of view. These can help to solve problems where participants have shared responsibility or a contribution to make. Often, however, full advantage is not taken of group settings. When used properly, group gatherings can be the best way to solve some problems.

When groups are useful

It is important to know when and when not to work in a group. The following checklist can help you decide. The more you answer 'Yes' to these questions, the more appropriate it is to use group problem solving.

■ Can the problem be defined in many different ways?

■ Is information from many different sources required?

- Is it a specialized problem?
- Does the problem have implications for many people?
- Are there likely to be many possible solutions?
- Is it a complex problem with many different aspects?
- Will a solution need to be agreed by others?

The deciding question is always: Are suitable and relevant people available to work together on this problem?

Success as a group

Problem solving can be complex and frustrating. It requires a careful manipulation of mental skills, and this is very susceptible to outside influence. When people are working together, they influence each other; group problem solving has to be managed very carefully if the best results are to be achieved.

Group problem solving has potential drawbacks as well as benefits. Some people working in a group may perceive the situation as competitive. Some may ignore what others are suggesting in their eagerness to express their own ideas. Others may want to conform to the consensus. Although agreement on ideas may be gained easily in a group setting, groups also tend to select and approve solutions quickly without exploring all the possibilities.

Meetings convened to solve problems are often directed ineffectively. There may be no designated leader to give direction to the discussion. Conversely, a strong leader or chairperson may exert inappropriate pressure on participants. In addition, many of the ideas aired may not be recorded, apart from official minutes and individual note-taking.

On the benefits side, group problem solving can generate a large number and wide variety of ideas. The shared decision making of a group can stimulate individuals to explore ideas they would not otherwise consider, and to challenge accepted ways of doing things. Working as a group can also result in more commitment to finding a solution and to its successful implementation. Communication is obviously improved.

Properly managed, and in the right situations, group problem solving results in better solutions. Various methods have been developed to make best use of group problem solving. These specify the role of the participants, including a leader, and the methods used by the group.

Participants should be selected to give the group a diversity of experience in various disciplines. Not all need be familiar with the problem area. All participants should understand the function of the group and what is expected of them. The methods used by the group should be designed to stimulate creativity and give direction to individual contributions, without the pressures and constraints of a normal meeting.

The skills involved in leading group problem solving are different from those used when chairing a meeting. The chair at a meeting normally judges which comments are relevant and which areas are worth exploring. Conversely, the leader in group problem solving is not there to make judgements; his or her primary role is to stimulate and record ideas. The precise responsibilities of the role vary slightly in different group techniques, but basically they include the following:

- briefing participants;
- keeping contributions flowing at a fast pace;
- ensuring everyone contributes;
- clarifying ideas when necessary;
- ensuring everyone sticks to the 'rules';

- prompting the group to explore new avenues;
- recording and displaying the group's ideas.

The leader's primary function is not to allow any participant to be put on the defensive. All participants must be free to concentrate on thinking up ideas, rather than on having to defend them.

Brainstorming

Brainstorming is the most popular technique designed specifically for group problem solving. It originated in an advertising agency, and generates a large number and a wide range of ideas in a comparatively short time. This is achieved by concentrating solely on idea generation, and on creating a light-hearted, free-wheeling atmosphere.

The number of people in a brainstorming session varies between five and 20, with an optimum of about 12. Everyone present contributes ideas, including the leader. Sessions are held in a room away from distractions, with a flip chart for recording ideas. Sessions can last for anything up to two hours, although the longer the session, the more difficult it is to sustain the flow of ideas.

The role of the leader in a brainstorming session begins with preparation: gaining a full understanding of the problem, selecting and inviting participants, and giving them a brief description of the problem to be solved. During the session, the leader stimulates, contributes and records ideas. It is the leader's job to enforce the four basic rules of brainstorming, which are the following:

- suspend judgement;
- free-wheel;
- cross-fertilize;
- quantity is good.

All the energy in a brainstorming session is directed towards producing ideas for solving the problem. There is no evaluation of ideas. The session consists of the following four stages:

1. Defining and discussing the problem. The problem is described briefly by someone with knowledge of the situation; enough information is given for the others to understand the problem, but not so much that it inhibits their ideas for a solution. This stage usually takes around five minutes.

2. Re-stating the problem. Group members re-state the problem, looking at it from different angles and phrasing it in terms of 'How to . . .?'. The leader writes these down. Throughout the session all ideas are numbered serially for easy identification later. Re-statement continues until all ideas are exhausted. This should result in at least 25 re-statements, often many more.

3. Warming up. At this stage it is useful to use an exercise (such as 'other uses for . . .') to get people in a free-wheeling frame of mind. This process is not recorded.

4. Brainstorming. One of the re-statements is selected, either by the leader or by voting. The leader writes it down on a new sheet of paper, re-phrased as 'In how many ways can we . . .?'. The leader reads the re-statement aloud and asks for ideas, writing them down as they are called out. When a sheet is full, it is displayed prominently on a wall to act as a stimulus to further ideas. When all ideas have been exhausted, another re-statement is selected, as remote as possible from the first, and the process is repeated. Three or four re-statements are treated in this way.

The leader can use various methods to stimulate the group, including repeating ideas as they are written down, asking for variations on an earlier idea, and using prompts such as 'who cares? Let's play with the idea', and 'tell me ways we could achieve that'.

When ideas dry up, the leader asks the group to select the wildest idea from the lists and to suggest useful variations. This is done a couple of times before the leader describes the evaluation process and ends the session.

Evaluation takes place on another day, once a list of all the ideas has been compiled. There are two methods of evaluation. It is either done by a small team from the original session, including the leader, or by all participants individually. Using both methods helps to prevent potentially useful ideas being discarded.

The list of ideas is sent to participants, who each vote for a small proportion of ideas they feel could be useful. They send the numbers of these ideas to the leader, who collates the results and discards those ideas with few votes. The team also meets to discuss the full list of ideas, using criteria of effectiveness (*see* page 28) to select the best ones. The two lists of remaining ideas are collated by the leader and the ideas with the highest number of votes are selected for further evaluation. At this stage, the ideas are examined to see how they could be modified and improved before they are rejected or accepted.

Not everyone has access to properly run group problem-solving sessions. However, we can all appreciate the need sometimes to get a wider perspective by collaborating with others. If you are aware of the potential pitfalls, you can gain some of the benefits of group problem solving through well-managed meetings. These do not offer the same potential for idea generation and cross-fertilization, but shared experience and knowledge can produce benefits.

41

6

CHOOSING THE BEST SOLUTION

When you have a number of possible solutions, each with a different mix of benefits and drawbacks, you need to evaluate them in order to identify the most effective. Even with only one solution, you must decide if it is acceptable and, if so, take the decision to implement it.

Identifying which solution will be most effective in achieving your objective is a complex decision-making process. It requires a methodical evaluation of all the options against the exact requirements of your ideal solution, identifying and comparing their relative values. Even then, your selection will often be a compromise between conflicting needs and the benefits and drawbacks of each solution.

Sometimes decision-making is influenced to varying extents, by subjective values. For example, the majority of people rely on personal preferences when choosing a holiday destination (and this is reasonable); similarly, most people rely heavily on past experience and gut feeling when asked to make a snap decision. However, we are so accustomed to using our own subjective values in decision-making that they can mislead us when an objective decision is required. Therefore, the opinions and preferences of those involved in a problem must be considered when evaluating solutions.

Evaluation can be divided into six stages:

1. deciding who to involve;
2. defining the 'ideal' solution;
3. eliminating unworkable solutions;
4. evaluating viable options;
5. assessing risks;
6. committing to a solution.

Deciding who to involve

There are many situations in which a solution may be chosen and implemented by one person, without anyone else being involved in the process. Sometimes you might consult other people out of personal regard for them, or because it is politic to do so. At other times, it may be essential – when you do not have the authority to act, for example, or when you need information, skills or knowledge from others.

Gaining the commitment of others may be integral to solving a problem. People affected can include those who have to agree to the solution, to live with it, to implement it or to provide the necessary resources. At work, this could include customers and suppliers, as well as employees.

A good way of gaining commitment is to involve people in the decision-making process, although this can have drawbacks. In particular, the process can become more complicated and protracted. You need to be sure that involving them is the best or only way to help you achieve your objective.

Defining the ideal solution

The acceptable or ideal solutions you have defined (*see* page 28) are inadequate to make an effective evaluation. Each solution may differ slightly or radically in the way and in the extent to which it achieves your various goals. To evaluate these effectively you need to construct a model that allows you to make measurable comparisons. Consider the outcomes required and the constraints within which you have to work.

Outcomes or results required

Outcomes include the benefits required in terms of the objective, as well as effectively dealing with obstacles/causes and, sometimes, gaining acceptance of the solution and/or its effects by other people. Depending on your objective, the desired outcome may be fixed (such as passing an examination), or flexible (for example, achieving the highest possible score in that examination).

Constraints

Constraints are generally specified as the limits of resources (time, space, money, materials, people), the minimum results acceptable, and the maximum disadvantages that can be tolerated.

Resources may be limited by what is available or what the problem justifies. Minimum acceptable results may be stated in absolute terms (such as achieving 100 per cent accuracy in quality control), or relative terms (such as achieving 100 per cent accuracy, *provided* it does not increase costs by more than 5 per cent). The maximum tolerable disadvantages are stated in terms of unacceptable costs in resources and of undesirable side-effects. Other factors may also represent a constraint, such as company policy dictating how certain issues are handled.

Here is a simple example of how an ideal solution might be defined:

Problem: reduce expenditure on stationery, from £1850 per month to under £1500 per month within four months. Results required:

- expenditure on stationery under £1500 per month (a 19 per cent reduction);

- prevention of wastage, misuse and pilfering of stationery;

- a simple administrative system.

Constraints:

- target to be achieved within four months;

- no additional administrative time beyond the current level, once the target has been achieved;

- supplier cannot be changed;

- a 12 per cent reduction in costs would be acceptable initially;

- a blatant 'policing' strategy will not be acceptable.

There are many different ways of achieving an ideal solution, each involving different benefits and drawbacks. One way to achieve a saving, for example, might be to distribute stationery regularly on a controlled basis; the risk is that sometimes people might be left without essential items.

Another solution might be to make people accountable for their stationery costs, but this could be viewed as petty, and involve extra paperwork.

It is often difficult to choose between solutions which have different disadvantages, and which the results required to differing extents. For example, would it be better to prevent wastage of stationery completely, and accept that this will require complex administration, or to achieve reduced wastage using a simpler system? Each outcome needs to be rated according to its relative value. This is done by selecting the most important outcome, giving it an arbitrary value (for example, five), and then rating all the others against this standard. In the stationery example, simplicity of administration might be given a value of five, while reduction in expenditure is rated four. Disadvantages are rated in a similar way, but with negative values according to their relative severity.

When the outcome of a particular course of action is uncertain, you need to estimate the probabilities of what will happen. Probability is expressed as a figure between zero and one, where zero is no probability and one is complete certainty. The probability of finding new customers through a mailshot, for example, may be 0.01 (one new customer for each 100 mailed), and through a personal visit 0.14 (14 new customers per 100 visits). Probabilities must also be calculated where costs and side-effects are uncertain.

Decisions are not always made by choosing the optimum mix of results. Instead, the following strategies may be used in certain situations:

■ Selecting any solution which achieves a minimum set of requirements. This approach could be used when there is insufficient time or information for a detailed or full evaluation.

46

- Giving preference to one particular evaluation criterion; for example, employing the person with the best telephone manner. This might be used when one criterion has particular significance and there is insufficient time or information for a full evaluation.

- Giving preference to solutions with minimal disadvantage on a particular criterion; for example, buying the make of popular car that shows minimum annual depreciation.

When you are ready to begin evaluating solutions, you can use the following three stages to reduce the time required for evaluation.

Eliminating unworkable solutions

Examine each solution in turn and reject those which do not meet all the constraints you have identified, such as financial cost and time. Record your reasons for rejection, so that you can check them later. Sometimes you can modify an otherwise unacceptable solution so that it comes within the constraints and can be evaluated further. In choosing a holiday, for example, you might find an alternative travel company that offers the same holiday at a more affordable price.

Evaluating viable options

Examine each of the remaining solutions to see how well they provide the outcomes required. The best fit for each outcome is given an arbitrary value (for example, five) and the others are valued relative to this standard. In choosing a holiday, you may have rated the availability of water-skiing as five in importance. One package holiday offers inclusive water-skiing so you give this particular package five, according to this measure.

As each solution is evaluated, the results can be recorded in a table. The value of each solution for each outcome desired is found by multiplying its fit against the relative value of each outcome. The inclusive holiday would rate 25 (five times five) on the water-skiing measure.

The disadvantages are also rated and given a negative value. The inclusive holiday might rate low on nightlife (minus three), which you gave a priority of four. So, that option rates a minus 12 (three times four) for nightlife.

The 'best' solution is the one with the highest aggregate score when all the outcomes and disadvantages have been evaluated.

Before moving to the next stage, check that your evaluation is accurate and that you have not omitted any relevant factors.

Assessing risks

The solution chosen by this stage offers the best balance of benefits versus drawbacks. Now you need to examine the possible risks associated with this solution. Are they acceptable and could they be minimized?

To assess risks you need to know what could go wrong, how likely it is to happen, and how severe the effects would be. Risks are most likely to arise from using inaccurate information during development and evaluation of solutions, and during implementation.

If you suspect any of the information you have used is unreliable, you should double-check. If your suspicions are confirmed, you must decide what implications it has for the likely success of the solution. For example, a company might have estimated that productivity would increase 15 per cent after the installation of new equipment. A review of the figures shows this to be nearer 8 per cent. Is the purchase still viable, given the reduced productivity gain?

You should also consider what could happen if the implementation of a solution does not go as planned. For example, what could be the effects of external factors, the people involved, the commitment of resources or slippage in the time schedule? Sometimes you need to draw up a rough plan for implementation (*see* Chapter 8) before you can determine the potential risks; for example, in terms of keeping to a time schedule.

For each risk you identify you need to calculate the probability of an undesirable outcome, and the severity of its effects. Then, if possible, you should build into your solution ways of minimizing these risks.

If the risks are unacceptable, and cannot be reduced by adapting the solution, that solution must be rejected and the next highest-scoring solution assessed. Continue this process until you find the best-rating solution involving acceptable risk.

Committing to a solution

Finally, take the decision to implement your chosen solution. The problem will remain unsolved unless you commit to taking action. At the same time you may need (or want) to gain approval for the implementation of the solution; this process is covered in Chapter 7.

7

GETTING A SOLUTION ACCEPTED

Once you have chosen a solution, you may need other people's co-operation, approval or authority before you can implement it. With routine problems, where people will know what is involved, you can simply tell them your decision. With complex and uncommon problems, and where major change or extensive use of resources is required, you must present your solution in detail. To do this effectively you need both to understand the reasons why people may oppose, and possibly reject, your solution, and to present that solution in a way that encourages their acceptance.

If you have involved relevant people in finding and evaluating solutions, you may already have their approval and commitment, but people involved in the solution will still need to have details of your plan for implementation. This is described in Chapter 8, but also forms part of your presentation of the solution for approval.

Reasons for opposition

You need to identify areas of possible opposition to your solution. Consider the following:

- how the solution could adversely affect the people involved;

- what they expect or need from the solution and what it will give them;

- their feelings about the nature of the problem and your solution;

- their relationship with, and perception of, you;

- what the solution requires of them.

However good a solution, the way it is presented to people involved or affected can determine whether it will succeed or fail. There are many reasons why people may oppose it, not all directly related to the ideas and actions involved.

People will scrutinize a solution more closely when it affects them in a major way, or when they have a good knowledge of the problem or of aspects of the solution. Simple differences of opinion may cause them to oppose your solution, unless you explain your reasoning clearly.

Lack of interest in the problem can create opposition from people who may feel you are wasting their time by involving them. Lack of knowledge of the problem area can also create opposition; people need sufficient information so that they understand the problem and the solution.

People's needs and expectations can influence their reaction to your proposal if, for example, it challenges their authority or creates extra work for them. Some people and organizations are resistant to change. A solution that involves considerable change may, therefore, encounter strong opposition, even when it is good and well presented. To overcome resistance, you need to emphasize the

51

benefits of the solution, and show how these can be achieved in practice.

Many people have an in-built suspicion of solutions that are highly innovative, or that yield high rewards by a simple method that seems too good to be true. Clear reasoning with supporting evidence should overcome this.

You can create opposition by not presenting your solution properly. You must ensure that you show that the benefits outweigh the disadvantages, that you have considered the side-effects and risks, and give adequate information, communicated effectively. An ill-timed solution can also meet with opposition; for example, it might be considered tactless to propose a solution that requires additional staff shortly after redundancies have been made.

Your relationship with those to whom you are presenting your solution, and what they feel about you, can have a significant influence on their response. These factors are complex and may have developed over a long period. At some time in the distant past you may have criticized or rejected someone else's ideas. When it is time to listen to your ideas, that person may still feel resentment. A young and enthusiastic manager, keen on applying the latest techniques, may encounter opposition from a more mature, traditional manager, who resents his or her progressive attitude.

Getting a good solution accepted (never try to sell a bad solution) is a matter of persuasive communication. Preparation is the key to success. Explore the possible reasons for opposition by analysing the problem, its solution and the people involved and affected by it. Once you know the likely reasons for opposition, you can include counters to these objections in your presentation. You will find that most of them can be avoided or overcome with a bit of common sense.

Preparing a presentation

You may present your solution verbally or in a written report, depending on the situation. If you have a choice, a meeting gives you the opportunity to get immediate feedback, and to respond persuasively to doubts and objections. A report gives you more control over the words you use and the effects they have. Most solutions requiring major changes or extensive use of resources will involve written reports at some stage.

To stand the best chances of success, you should do the following:

- anticipate opposition and incorporate counter-measures in your presentation;

- give people the opportunity to explain their objections, otherwise you may give the impression that you are trying to gloss over flaws in your solution;

- get people involved – explain how the solution will affect them, or how they will have a role in implementation;

- appeal to people's self-interest, making a point of telling them at the beginning how they will benefit from your solution;

- justify the resources you want to use; give hard facts about the return on investment;

- show enthusiasm for your solution; it can be infectious;

- be prepared to make concessions, especially when people expect to negotiate;

- choose a good time for your presentation, when people are least likely to be distracted by other problems, imminent holidays, or break times.

The way you present information is crucial to success. Aim to make your presentation as clear and as simple as the subject allows, and to the point. You want everyone to understand it easily. When the issues are complex, concentrate on the key points. Leave the more complicated points for later discussion, or include them in an appendix to a report. Tell people that this is what you intend to do.

In verbal presentations, the order in which you present your ideas is particularly important. If you reveal your solution at the outset, for example, people may foresee disadvantages and raise objections before you have the chance to explain how you will handle the situation. First impressions are difficult to change. The following steps will help you structure your talk clearly:

- state the overall objective in solving the problem;

- describe the constraints on the situation;

- briefly describe all the results you felt were required and their relative importance;

- briefly state all the options you considered, without saying which you have chosen;

- describe the measures you have used to evaluate solutions and their relative importance;

- state which option you have chosen, explaining why it is the best solution, and describe the associated risks you have identified;

- explain how the solution will be implemented;

- state how the results will be identified and measured.

Many people are anxious about making verbal presentations, but this can be eased by thorough preparation and rehearsal.

Written reports can vary from a single-page outline to a large bound volume of 100 pages or more, but they should never contain unnecessary information. The content, structure, writing style and layout should all aim to make the information easy to understand, while providing a persuasive argument.

Seek advice in one of the many books available to help you make effective presentations and to write good reports.

If your solution is rejected

It is not uncommon for ideas to be rejected, particularly when they are innovative, involve major change, or require extensive use of resources. If your idea is rejected, you have a number of options:

1. check that you presented your idea effectively; if not, it may be worth re-presenting it, if you have the opportunity;

2. consider whether you can present the idea to someone else who can authorize its acceptance, or seek to win over someone who will benefit most from your decision and who could bring pressure to bear on the decision-makers;

3. improve your solution to overcome the objections and then re-present it;

4. look for another solution, bearing in mind the reasons why your first solution was rejected.

Trying to get a solution accepted can be frustrating and difficult. This is true especially where you are encroaching on other people's territory, or when there is no existing yardstick against which to measure the likely outcome. If you firmly believe in your idea, persevere. It will often pay off.

8

IMPLEMENTING A SOLUTION

There are three stages in finally resolving a problem:

1. planning and preparing to act;
2. implementing and monitoring the plan; and
3. reviewing the outcome.

With many problems, this process requires careful attention to detail.

Planning and preparation

The more important the problem, or the more complex the actions required to solve it, the more planning and preparation is required. First, you need to construct a plan of action showing what actions are required, their timing and the resources needed. Then you have to arrange for the necessary resources to be made available at the right time, including the people involved.

A plan of action

Unless the problem is simple or routine, you need to construct a detailed plan of action for the implementation of the solution. This involves systematically identifying and recording the actions required, and their timing, the resources required, the method by which implementation will be kept on course, the management of the actions, and the checking of the plan.

To specify what must be done and the expected outcome, follow these steps:

1. state your overall objective;

2. list the individual goals in the order in which they must be achieved in order to reach the objective;

3. identify those actions required to achieve each goal, determine the sequence in which they need to be carried out, and record them alongside each goal;

4. define, in measurable terms, what a successful outcome will be for each action and add the details to the plan.

The order of the various actions is determined by a number of factors. Sometimes it is necessary to complete one action or set of actions before another can begin, like laying a foundation before building a wall. Actions also have to run consecutively when they each use the same resource to capacity (for example, two separate walls and only one bricklayer).

It is wise to use a diagram to represent the sequence of actions, and how they contribute to the overall objective. This helps to show how the actions interact and to reveal areas of possible conflict. Actions should be fitted together as closely as possible, to prevent wastage of resources, while allowing some margin for overrun. To do this, you need to prepare a time schedule for the actions.

First, identify the time required to complete each action. By representing this information on a diagram, you can see clearly at what stage, relative to the start time, each action will commence and finish, and determine the total time required to achieve the objective. Simple plans can be represented by a chart with horizontal bars showing the sequence and duration of the actions. More complex plans require a more flexible structure, like a chain diagram or a flowchart (*see* page 26). A diagram helps you arrange the actions in a way which makes the best use of time and other resources. For example, if two actions each require two days' use of an excavator, which can be hired only on a weekly basis, these actions should be scheduled for the same week.

When completed, the diagram also shows which actions are most crucial to complete on time (for example, a flooded site must be drained before the excavators move in), and how a delay or time-saving in completing one action will affect all the others (for example, bad weather may delay the commencement of one action, and have a knock-on effect).

Do not underestimate the time it will take to complete an action. You need to accommodate delays and unforeseen obstacles.

Resources required

Resources include people, money, materials, space and information, as well as time. Consider each resource in turn in relation to all the actions required.

Time. The importance of time is easily overlooked. Consider whose time is required. Will this time be spent within normal working hours or when people are normally available?

People. Human resources may be required from within

58

and from outside a company. Friends and family may be involved in resolving personal situations. Consider how many people will be required. What skills, qualities and knowledge are needed? When and where will the people be required? Will they be available for the length of time required? What briefing and training will they need to be able to carry out their tasks effectively?

Money. Define the financial resources required, as follows:

- how much and in what form; for example, cash, cheque, foreign currency;

- the source; for example, bank, earnings, local government;

- whether its use will be compatible with the source; for example, in the case of a business development grant;

- whether it needs to be repaid, and when;

- whether it will be recouped, and how and when; for example, through cost savings;

- whether there will be additional costs, such as interest or handling charges;

- whether the costs of all other resources have been included.

Materials. These may fall into a number of categories, including consumables, raw materials and equipment (all for temporary or permanent use). You need to define the following.

- What type of materials are needed?

- If capital equipment, how will it be financed; for example, on lease, with a loan?

- What are the specifications, including quality and size?

- What wastage is likely to occur?

- What quantities are required?
- Will transport and handling (human and mechanical) be required?

Space. You need to consider the following questions.

- How much space and where?
- Should the space be of a particular type (for example, covered, or with amenities), or of particular dimensions?
- When will the space be needed, and for how long?

Information. This may form a part of the human resource (for example, expert advice or skills), or it may be some item such as a rented mailing list. You will need to decide on the following.

- What specific information is required?
- Is it available from within the organization or does it need to be bought in?
- Where specifically is it available?
- When and where will it be required?
- For how long will it be required?

Do not underestimate the resources required. A shortage could disrupt implementation or incur heavy penalties, such as having to pay consultants for doing nothing while they are waiting for the installation of a piece of equipment. Sometimes you have to adapt your plan of action to suit the availability of resources.

Next, draw up a schedule of resources showing how and when they will be requested, and from whom, when and where they are to be delivered or made available and, where relevant, for how long they will be required. Allow sufficient time between ordering and the required delivery date.

Keeping on course

You have considered areas of risk and possible side-effects in constructing and evaluating your solution. You have adapted the solution in order to minimize the adverse consequences. Now you need to identify everything that could go wrong during implementation, and devise counter measures.

There are certain factors in any plan of action which make it more susceptible to something going wrong. To identify these, and to make provision for dealing with them, examine your plan step by step, as follows.

Are there areas where, for example:

- timing is crucial, and a deadline could be missed if there is a delay;

- two or more activities coincide, and might interfere with each other;

- there is heavy reliance on the co-operation and efforts of people, and it is crucial for them to perform as required;

- external factors could affect the actions required (as could the weather), or the effectiveness of the results (for example, a change in product popularity)?

You need to analyse and evaluate the consequences. First, define what the effects are likely to be if something goes wrong, and then decide what is the probability (low, medium or high) of this happening.

- Find ways to spot trouble as early as possible.

- Devise counter measures either to prevent the cause or minimize its effects.

- Incorporate the ways of spotting trouble, and the counter measures into your plan.

This sounds complicated, but it is mostly common sense. You can only afford to omit minor adverse consequences with a low probability, otherwise you risk jeopardizing the rest of the plan.

Managing the actions

You need to specify how implementation will be monitored and controlled. People must be led and managed, their progress measured at specific intervals, and action taken to correct any variation from the plan. The following steps help to specify how to manage the implementation.

1. Identify actions requiring on-the-job supervision and monitoring.
2. Identify points at which progress should be measured; for example, upon completion of individual goals or at critical phases.
3. Specify exactly what results are expected at these stages.
4. Specify how and by whom results will be measured. Specify in your plan actions to be taken to correct any shortfall in results.

The stages you identify for measuring progress are, in effect, deadlines for achieving specific results. State these as a specific time or date in the overall time schedule. Also, make provision to monitor the solution once it has been implemented, so that any unforeseen consequences arising in the longer term can be detected.

Finally, you need to check your plan. It represents a critical stage in ensuring efficient implementation and must be accurate and thorough.

Arranging resources

Once you know all about the resources required, and have drawn up a detailed and thorough plan, it is a relatively simple matter to arrange for these to be available at the right time and place. This includes the selection, briefing and training of the people involved in implementation.

Each person, selected for their skills, qualities or knowledge, will need a clear plan of what they have to do, the results expected of them and their responsibilities. Briefing them is often the final step before a plan is implemented. As with any other type of communication, it must be planned and executed carefully. Sometimes, people will require special training for their role.

Implementing and monitoring the plan

Once action is initiated, supervising and monitoring activity ensures that people carry out their tasks efficiently, and allows corrective action to be taken if there is any deviation from the plan.

Taking corrective action may mean implementing the appropriate counter measure laid down in the plan, or taking unplanned action to counter unforeseen problems. If time has been lost in completing one activity, for example, other activities may have to be completed more quickly than planned in order to meet a deadline. Minor problems that are unlikely to recur may not require any action.

Major faults in the plan may mean that it is necessary to abandon implementation if no appropriate corrective action is possible.

Reviewing the outcome

When the plan has been completed and the solution implemented, you should analyse and measure its success. This tells you how effective the solution has been and how useful it will be in solving similar problems in the future.

You can take additional action if necessary and also learn from your mistakes.

To measure success you simply compare the outcome of the actions taken with what you were trying to achieve. Sometimes you have to measure the results regularly over a period of time to see if the initial results are being maintained.

Further action may be desirable if initial results cannot be maintained without intervention, or if the goalposts have moved and the results do not meet the new targets. To decide what further action is required, you have to define new objectives and any associated obstacles – this can produce a new problem for you to solve, and thus the process has come full circle.